Wonder And Whimsy

A collection of poems inspired by the simple
beauty of everyday life

Sydney Fogelberg

BookLeaf
Publishing

India | USA | UK

Made with ❤ on the BookLeaf Publishing Platform
www.bookleafpub.in
www.bookleafpub.com

Dedication

To the people who see beauty in ordinary things.

Preface

This collection of poems was inspired by reflections on love, life, and finding joy and beauty in the mundane and ordinary moments of life. I hope this book inspires you to notice the beauty and wonder all around you.

Acknowledgements

The creation of this book would not be possible without the encouragement and love from some very special people. Thank you Chris for carefully reading each and every poem of mine and for recognizing my poems as something special. Thank you for supporting this dream of writing my very own poetry book, it means the world to me. Kuhu, thank you for the times you spent listening to me read these poems out loud and confirming that I have written something that will touch hearts. And thank you for being such a beautiful friend to me. Maddie, thank you for encouraging me to write even when I didn't feel like it. Your excitement for reading my poems inspired me to keep writing. Each of you has been an inspiration for my poetry, and I am deeply thankful for the love and joy you have added to my life.

1. Spontaneity

While sometimes nice to have an orderly plan
there is a joy in letting a moment happen all on its own
accord
like when you're in the kitchen with people you love
and all of the sudden a dance party breaks out
or going for a last minute walk with friends on a chilly
night
sharing stories and laughing until your stomach hurts
hearts warmed despite cool wind
sometimes the very best and beautiful moments happen
in spontaneity

2. Sunshine

Seeing you
is like seeing sunshine
after a week of clouds

3. A walk in the rain

I love walks in the rain
the way the streets are quiet
and the grass looks greener
the comforting pitter patter of raindrops on my umbrella
the chilly wind that makes my cheeks rosy
time well spent observing things I otherwise wouldn't
have noticed
if the sun were shining

4. My name

I never thought my name was special
until I heard it come out of your mouth
and suddenly
it was poetry to my ears

6. Whimsy and Wonder

Today I saw three little girls stooped down
 beholding something in fascination
when I joined their huddle
I noticed they were completely content
playing with a beetle and a purple flower petal
and it made me question
as we're growing up, how do we lose that sense of
childlike whimsy and wonder?
when did we lose the power to be fascinated by small
and unimportant things?
in a world that beckons us to busyness
and tells us to grow up too fast
make the choice to awaken and delight that inner child
living in each of our souls

8. Broken hearted blessings

The blessing of a broken heart
is that it gives you the opportunity to put the pieces back
together
like an artist creating a mosaic
little by little, piece by piece
until the broken shards come together
in a way that is more beautiful and resilient than it was
before

9. Light

Step outside
throw your head back and grin towards the sky
as the golden, honey sweet sunshine pours over your
face
brings warmth to your body
and floods your soul with light

11. The people we see in passing

Have you ever stopped to think
that the barista making your coffee
the mother with the screaming baby just trying to get
through her shopping list
the homeless man you drive by on your way to work

the people we see in passing
all have a history
each with their own struggles and joys
dreams and disappointments
inside each of us is a little universe
not easily discovered by a glance
a depth that, if we're lucky, a few people in our lifetime
are willing to dive into

so I encourage you
to really look at your fellow humans
and see beyond what is visible to the eye
see the value that is innately woven into every person
the beautiful and broken parts of their stories

for it might open our hearts to notice
that even with our differences

we are all united by our humanity
doing our best to live and love in an unkind world
and in this noticing
let your heart be filled with love and compassion
for our fellow humans who walk with us
making this journey on earth a little less lonely

12. Rainstorm kind of love

Have you ever been out for a walk and all of the sudden
got caught up in a pouring rain?
one minute you're strolling along minding your business
and the next you're completely drenched from rain that
came out of nowhere
that is the way I fell in love with you
all of the sudden, unexpectedly, no warning
it hit me like a surprise rainstorm
no place for me to take shelter, no escaping
I just stood there out in the open
defenseless
and let the rain fall on my skin
it's all I could do

13. Beauty in the unknown

As I walk up the winding roads of my Himalayan
hometown
I am reminded that nothing in life
is ever perfectly straightforward
embrace the mystery
of not knowing exactly what is around the bend
for it might just be breathtakingly beautiful

14. Soul awakening

When you walk into the room
my soul awakens
like the sun slowly rising over the mountains
and quietly filling the earth
with the gift of light

15. New lifetime

How is it possible that a year ago feels like a lifetime
ago?
maybe it's the new surroundings I'm living in
how I now feel like a foreigner in the town where I grew
up
or maybe the new friendships I've made
that have taught me how to be loved again
and have opened up parts of my heart
I didn't know existed
maybe it's the difficult times I went through
that made me stronger and more resilient

As I reflect on the past year
I can see that so many parts of my old life have died
and new and beautiful things have started growing in
their place
and I realize
maybe this is the beginning
of a new lifetime for me

16. The moments we rush by

What if
instead of rushing to get out the door in the morning
you took a moment
to sit by the window
and let the first rays of morning light
warm your hands and awaken tired eyes
what if
instead of pouring your coffee in a to go cup
and restlessly drinking it in traffic
you poured it into your favorite mug
savoring it
sip by sip
noticing the bold and bitter flavors
as they dance across your tongue
what if
instead of mindlessly scrolling on your phone at the
dinner table
you looked into the eyes and hearts of the people you
love
and felt genuinely thankful for their presence in your life
what if
the moments we rush by
are really the moments that make life worth living

17. Smaller acts

I don't see much great love in grand gestures
but in the way you quietly understand my thoughts
before I even say a word
how you make my morning coffee
just the way I like it
how we can sit together in comfortable silence
content and secure in each other's presence

to me
the most thoughtful and beautiful love
is expressed
day by day
in smaller acts

18. Perspective

As I approach the sink full of dishes
I'm not frustrated that I'll be here for some time
scrubbing and scraping

for all I can think of
is the soul-filling time spent
cooking
eating
laughing
doing life with people I love

and for that
I am thankful to the pile of dishes
and the memories they created

19. Wisdom from seeds

Maybe we should take wisdom from seeds
how they trust in the process
of being hidden beneath the earth
taking root
unhurriedly sprouting from the ground
and slowly reaching toward the sun
maybe seeds understand one thing better than we do
that beautiful things take time to grow

20. I think I loved you once before

When I'm with you
I feel nostalgic for a time I never even lived in
and it makes me wonder
if I loved you in another lifetime

21. What is Home?

Some may say that home is the place where four walls meet
the space that is a sanctuary from the world outside
others might say that home is a person
the one whose presence gives you peace
even when your mind is twirling with doubts

some may feel the solace of home as they lay beneath the trees
watching the branches sway and clouds drift by
maybe the feeling of home comes from a meal lovingly cooked by your mother
or from walking the familiar streets of the town where you grew up

maybe home rests in the thoughts of those
who lovingly think of you
or maybe in your traveling to a new place
you find an unexpected sense of belonging that feels like home

all I know is that my heart has felt home in all these things
and I wonder if throughout our lives

our hearts quietly lead us to the people
places
the moments
that feel like home

22. You don't have to tell me you love me

I don't need you to say "I love you"
to know that you do
I can see it in the way the corner of your mouth lifts
ever so slightly
when your eyes meet mine
I can feel it in the way your thumb slowly traces my
jawline
like you're admiring a precious and rare work of art
I can feel it when you say my name
and it comes out of your mouth
sounding like a prayer
all I know
is that if you never again told me you loved me
I would know deep in my bones
that you do

23. Everyday Miracles

Waking in the morning to the sweet sound of birdsong

taking a deep breath

and feeling the steady rhythm of your heartbeat

listening to a song that resonates with your soul

laughing with someone who appreciates your humor

holding a hand that fits perfectly into yours

each of these is an everyday miracle
if we open our eyes to see them as such

24. Favorite song

You are like listening to my
favorite song
I could hear it
over and over again
and it would never get old

25. Just Be

Sometimes when I am looking up into the depths of the
starry night sky
or admiring the majestic snow capped peaks of the
Himalayas in the distance
I become aware of how tiny my presence is in the
universe

a gentle reminder

that the world does not revolve around me
a reminder
to surrender my desire for control

and just be

content to bear witness to this wide and wonder-filled
world
and the magic it has to offer
those who notice

26. Awakening

This morning when I opened my window
I braced myself for the cold air
to meet my skin and shock my senses
into awakening

instead

I was greeted by a warm and gentle breeze
that felt as though the earth was breathing
a sigh of relief
that at last
winter has surrendered to spring
an invitation to all living things
to open their sleepy eyes
and once again
begin to bloom

www.ingramcontent.com/pod-product-compliance
Lightning Source LLC
La Vergne TN
LVHW041254200726

843507LV00013B/2971